This book is a
Gift

From

To

On the occassion of

Date

GRACE *to*

Olu B. Olumuyiwa

LasouchPublishing.com

GRACE TO SERVE

Published by:

LASOUCH PUBLISHING: 11355 Richmond Ave, Houston TX, 77082, US.

+1 (917) 594-7014, +2348058092923

www.lasouchpublishing.com

ISBN-13: 9798429760278

Unless otherwise indicated, all Scripture quotations are taken from the New King James Version of the Bible.

Table of Contents

Table of Contents

DEDICATION

This book is dedicated to those who are currently working, volunteering, serving and labouring in the kingdom of God in spirit and in truth as well as others who would join before Christ returns.

APPRECIATION

I like to appreciate my Lord and Savior through the Holy Spirit for dropping the whole content and the idea in my spirit with the simple instruction to put it into writing.

I also like to appreciate the support of my wife and son for standing by me through the whole process.

To my parents, Deacon Abraham and Deaconess Dorcas Somuyiwa for bringing me up in the way of the Lord. To my siblings and their family members for their prayers and support all the way.

To my pastor and his wife – Pastor Bayo and Pastor (Mrs) Toun Fadugba for believing in the gift of God upon my life to teach the Word of God in spirit and truth.

8

Appreciation

To the following people for their reviews, support, contributions and prayers while writing this book. Remi Folarin, Pastor Seyi Olumuyiwa, Dr. Funmilayo Salami Dr. Judipat Obiora, Pastor Leke Banjo, Pastor Dayo Aina, Minister Tomi Favor Alesh and the entire DCH family.

INTRODUCTION

The turn of events around the world today calls for a deeper reflection as to the true essence of life and how we live it. From the breakout of the global pandemic to extreme weather conditions, floods, serious storms and fire outbreaks, it is clear that we are living in *"the last of the last days."*

However, one thing that has remained constant in all these is the abundance of the grace of God! He has indeed been faithful and we have cause to return all the glory to Him. We thank God for His protection and for keeping us all as vessels He will use for such a time as this.

In this book *"Grace to Serve"*, I explore the subject of kingdom service from a standpoint of the grace of God. I show you through scriptural accounts how that God doesn't accept everything done in the name of service to Him! It has to be done by grace to gain His approval because grace is the vehicle for acceptable service.

I bring my decades of experience walking with the Lord to bear as I share deep truths about the true meaning of grace, examples of Christian services, and the place of grace in leading a life of relevance in the Kingdom of God, with rewards that begin right here on earth.

You will discover the difference between being a son and a servant in the kingdom of God and also learn what is the missing ingredient in the lives of those who would end up hearing the Lord say to them *"... I never knew you; depart from Me, you who practice lawlessness!"* (Matt. 7:23)

I also elaborate on fifteen distinguishing attributes of gracious service and show you how these principles apply to your Christian walk today. Something very interesting about this book as well is that each point is laced around with personal prayers and declarations as well.

Whether you are a veteran kingdom worker, church leader, backslidden believer or a New Convert; this book will help you discover your purpose from the womb of grace. It will help you begin to shine effortlessly in all facets of life as you give God acceptable service that stands the test of time moving forward.

Read this book if you look forward to hearing *"well done thou good and faithful servant"* from the Lord!

Olu B. Olumuyiwa
Associate Pastor, R.C.C.G.
Dominion Chapel Houston
Texas, USA.

CHAPTER ONE

UNDERSTANDING GRACE

CHAPTER ONE
SUMMARY

- What is the meaning of Grace?
- Examples of Christian Service
- What is the "Grace to Serve"?

"Not that we are sufficient of ourselves to think of anything as being from ourselves, but our sufficiency is from God,"

2 Cor 3:5

CHAPTER ONE

UNDERSTANDING GRACE

The subject of the grace of God is probably one of the most controversial ones in the body of Christ today. People either don't understand it at all or they have a perverted view of it. That is why, after being born again and serving in the church of Jesus in several capacities over the years, I have come to appreciate the honour to serve and worship in a place where we can freely teach about grace.

I know some Christian circles where you don't talk about grace. In some others, it's 50% grace and 50% law.

So I count it an honour to worship in a place where we can teach about grace without fear of being blacked out or reprimanded.

What is the Meaning of Grace?

While our focus in this book is the *"Grace to Serve"*, I don't want to make any assumptions that you already understand what grace is. So I believe it will be great to take our sail from understanding what grace is first.

In simple terms, grace is the undeserved, unearned and unmerited favour of God. You don't work for it, you don't fight for it and you didn't merit it. It is something that God just decided to give to you without making any demand from you.

Also, one definition that I always like to give is found in John 3:16.

> *"For God so loved the world that He gave His only begotten Son, that whoever believes in Him should not perish but have everlasting life."*

John 3:16

Grace is the expression of the love and goodness of God. You know, God could have given us a long list of

16

things we must do to qualify for His love but He didn't. He didn't wait for us to do something good or nice before sending Jesus Christ to die for us.

You are probably familiar with the term *"entry qualification"*. Whether it is a job you are applying for or a college you are applying to study in, certain criteria must be met to qualify for the position in view. If you don't meet those requirements, you don't get admitted but once you meet up, you expect to be granted the position on merit.

Grace is not like that. It is different in that it does not require a qualification from the recipient before they are granted access! The Bible says *"But God demonstrates His own love toward us, in that while we were still sinners, Christ died for us."* (Rom 5:8)

That is the highest level of the expression of the Love of God and it's all based on the grace of God.

Now, since we are talking about the *"grace to serve,"* you might be asking, *"what exactly does it mean to serve,"* right? The services we are talking about here are the ones that have to do with the kingdom of God. Here we are talking about Christian Service.

What then is a Christian Service? It is simply anything that you do or any service that you render in the name of the Lord and to advance the kingdom of God. This could be you fulfilling the call of God upon your life or you expressing the gift of God upon your life.

In other words, the fact that someone is a Christian and serves in one capacity or the other doesn't mean that service qualifies to be described as *"Christian Service"* The focal point is that the service has to be for the kingdom of God!

Christian Service is therefore different from the personal ambitions or desires of the Christian. It is that service that comes as a result of what you (the Christian) have decided to do for the Lord Jesus Christ after being saved by God through grace. It is you living for the fulfilment of the will and purpose of God rather than running your show!

Examples of Christian Service.

In one of His teachings, Jesus gave an analogy of how the kingdom functions and what true Christian Service looks like.

"When the Son of Man comes in His glory, and all the holy angels with Him, then He will sit on the throne of His glory. All the nations will be gathered before Him, and He will separate them one from another, as a shepherd divides his sheep from the goats. And He will set the sheep on His right hand, but the goats on the left. Then the King will say to those on His right hand, 'Come, you blessed of My Father, inherit the kingdom prepared for you from the foundation of the world: for I was hungry and you gave Me food; I was thirsty and you gave Me drink; I was a stranger and you took Me in; I was naked and you clothed Me; I was sick and you visited Me; I was in prison and you came to Me."

Matt 25:31-36

Notice that Jesus spoke about feeding the hungry, giving drink to the thirsty, sheltering the stranded, clothing the naked, nursing the sick and visiting the imprisoned. In other words, he referred to all sorts of humanitarian services but stressed that when you do them in the name of God, it becomes much more.

Once anything is done in the name of the Lord, no matter how seemingly unimportant it may be, it becomes Divine Service and attracts Divine Rewards both in this world and in eternity as well.

So from the above scripture, you would realize that doing good for people, giving to people, going to prison to preach and all are the works of the kingdom and they have rewards attached to them.

What is the "Grace to Serve"?

When we talk about Grace to Serve, we are referring to that simple, unmerited ability or enablement given to us as believers to do exactly what God has called us to do for His kingdom. It is God working in you both to will and to do of His good pleasure. It is divine enablement for a supernatural performance of a divinely appointed task. Paul puts it so succinctly when he said;

"Not that we are sufficient of ourselves to think of anything as being from ourselves, but our sufficiency is from God,"

2 Cor 3:5

"Not that we are fit (qualified and sufficient in ability) of ourselves to form personal judgments or to claim or count anything as coming from us, but our power and ability and sufficiency are from God."

2 Cor. 3:5 [AMPC]

20

No matter what it is we do or how proficient we become at it, Paul says it is not as though we are qualified, sufficient, or capable in ourselves. We don't have enough skill or experience to claim anything as coming from us. Rather our power and ability are from God!

Grace is that power, ability and sufficiency that God supplies us to render kingdom service to Him. So in the following chapters of this book, we are going to examine in detail, the attributes of *"Gracious Service."* We will consider what it means to serve by grace and how you can plug into that realm to fulfil your God-given assignment in life. To help you better understand this concept of grace for service, we will be studying what I call the *"Principles of Gracious Service."*

CHAPTER TWO

PRINCIPLES OF GRACIOUS SERVICE (1)

CHAPTER TWO SUMMARY

- The Principle of your Calling.
- The Principle of Obedience
- The Grace for Humility

Therefore, since we are receiving a kingdom which cannot be shaken, let us have grace, by which we may serve God acceptably with reverence and godly fear.

Heb 12:28

CHAPTER TWO

PRINCIPLES OF GRACIOUS SERVICE (1)

Our theme scripture for this study is Hebrews 12:28 which says:

> *"Therefore, since we are receiving a kingdom which cannot be shaken, let us have grace, by which we may serve God acceptably with reverence and godly fear."*

Heh 12:28

Let me paint the background of this scripture to you for a moment. The writer was writing to Jewish people who were used to the works of the law. As far as they were concerned, salvation and acceptability before the Lord was always a function of works. They had to do something to gain God's acceptance and pardon. However, in Christ Jesus, things have changed and most of them were not aware.

So the writer communicates here intending to point the people to the new order. He was telling them to receive the grace of God after which they can now serve God. Then their services can become acceptable. In other words, if you really want to serve God with humility and reverence, then you need to do it with grace.

From this verse of scripture, you will notice that grace can be redefined as the key to rendering "acceptable" service to God. That is why there is nothing wrong with waking up every day and receiving the grace of God. The grace is massively available and is ours to receive daily.

2 Important Notes on the Grace of God

Before we delve into the principles of Gracious Service, there are two things I will like to point out about the grace of God.

1) You Can Grow In It

"You, therefore, beloved, since you know this beforehand, beware lest you also fall from your own steadfastness, being led away with the error of the wicked; but grow in the grace and knowledge of our Lord and Savior Jesus Christ."

2 Pet 3:17-18

Peter, in referring to the teachings of Paul mentioned that the message of grace that Paul preached was something that many struggled with and stumbled in their walk with God. He, therefore, admonished the Church to beware of self-steadfastness.

He warned them to beware of the confidence in self which is the error of the wicked. Rather, they should endeavour to grow in grace and the knowledge of our Lord Jesus Christ. That means, instead of trying to please or serve God in your strength, growing in grace would yield better results with God.

That is, no matter what level of grace you operate in right now, it is possible to increase therein by growing in the knowledge of Jesus Christ as our Lord and Savior. This is the key to advancing from one level of grace to another and thereby increasing in effectiveness in your service to the Lord.

So as we begin to look at the principles of gracious service, it is okay to identify areas you need to grow in. It is also in order to aspire for more and more grace in a particular area. It is therefore my prayer, that as you read through, the Lord will grant you increased grace to serve more acceptably in Jesus name.

2) You Can Ask For It

Now that we see that we can grow in grace, the second important thing I want you to note about grace is that you can ask for it. In fact, you should ask for it!

You know some extremists believe that they already have all the grace of God they need and don't need to pray or ask for it but they are wrong. The Bible teaches us that there is nothing wrong with asking for grace.

> *"Let us therefore come boldly to the throne of grace, that we may obtain mercy and find grace to help in time of need."*

Heb 4:16

If we already had all the grace we need, God won't be asking us to come to the throne of grace, right? In fact, he uses the expression *"come boldly ..."* because God doesn't want us tiptoeing or fidgetting about it. He wants us to be bold about coming and asking for grace because that is part of our benefits of redemption in Christ.

If at any point in life you discover that the execution of your God-given assignment seems farfetched or unattainable, that is the time to remember that you can be bold enough to ask for grace. When life feels like you have come to a stop and exhausted all your ideas and strategies for fulfilling your kingdom mandate, remember that there is already the opportunity to come boldly and receive grace (divine enablement for supernatural fulfilment of assignment)

With these two notes out of the way, we can now begin to look at the principles of gracious service.

Principle #1: The Principle of your Calling

One thing we must understand as children of God is that the moment we received the gospel message and became saved, we embraced a calling. The term church in itself means *"the called-out ones."* So when anyone comes to Christ and becomes a member of the Church of Jesus Christ, he is automatically one of the called-out ones.

That means there is no room for "floor membership" in the Church of Jesus Christ. Every one of us has been called for something. We just need to discover what it is and commit ourselves to doing that thing.

Where I currently worship, for example, we have over 70 ministries. So no matter who you are and what your calling is, there is always somewhere for you to serve. There is a place for you in the kingdom of God and you want to key into that at once.

The principle of your calling says that every call is delivered through the wing of grace. You can't call yourself. If truly it is God that called you, the day you were called, you were "graced." It is like you were given birth to by the womb of grace. That is why you discover your calling; you don't initiate it.

PRAYER:

Lord, I know you have called me for a purpose by your grace, help me not to fail by trusting in your grace all the way, in Jesus name

Principle #2: The Principle of Obedience

In my years of walking with God, I have discovered that one of the reasons many people hesitate to obey the call or assignment of God for their lives is that they are scared of making mistakes. They don't want to disappoint God, themselves and the world, so they dillydally on and on. What they fail to understand is that no one was ever called or assigned a task in the kingdom because they felt fit for the job.

Those who appear fit became so because they took advantage of the grace to serve. Dear friend, you need to understand that it is easier to obey the voice of God when you know that there is grace to serve. The principle of obedience states that it is easier to obey when we understand that there is help (grace) to obey.

> *"Through Him we have received grace and apostleship for obedience to the faith among all nations for His name,"*

Rom 1:5

There is such a thing as *"grace for obedience to the faith"* This is the hidden truth behind the lives of those who seem to always find it easy to obey the Lord. They have received and taken advantage of this grace for obedience.

The Book of Acts further explains the concept of obedience to the faith in a way that shows us the role of grace in its occurrence.

"Then the word of God spread, and the number of the disciples multiplied greatly in Jerusalem, and a great many of the priests were obedient to the faith."

Acts 6:7

You will agree that if there is any group that was averse to the gospel of Christ, it was the Jews and their priests in particular. So how do you explain how priests later signed up for the same faith for which they crucified Jesus? What lecture of human wisdom could anyone have given them to change their minds? What religious presentation could the most eloquent speaker have made to make that switch in their perspective?

It is only the grace that leads to obedience of the faith that gives that kind of result. Now, guess what? That grace doesn't only lead unbelievers into salvation, it also enables believers to obey the word as it concerns their services to the Lord.

PRAYER:

Lord, I receive the grace to obey you with fear and shame in Jesus name

Principle #3: The Grace for Humility

The kingdom of God functions by special principles which may be different from the kingdom of the world. One of such principles is the principle of humility. The Bible says;

> *"But He gives more grace. Therefore He says: "God resists the proud, But gives grace to the humble."*

James 4:6

The scripture reveals that when a person is proud, God makes it a point of duty to resist them! There is just something about His personality that doesn't gel with a proud person at all. However, to the humble, God gives grace!

In the place of service, humility is one of the keys that unlock the door to a higher level of grace. If you ever want to enjoy more of God, it will have to come by grace and that grace is only directed towards the humble.

So when you begin to do extraordinary things, remember that it is the grace of God at work and not you. The more you release the glory to God, the more you receive grace to do more. Don't let pride take over your life.

God is never in lack of resources. He can use anyone so it is an opportunity to be used by Him. David was a professional guy but he knew he couldn't rely on his proficiency or the stones alone. He was willing to rely on God when he told Goliath "the battle is the Lord's" and "I come to you in the name of the Lord" That might be one of the reasons why he picked up only five stones. Don't allow pride to take over you.

PRAYER:

Dear Lord God, I receive the daily wisdom and understanding to remain humble as you multiply your grace upon my life in Jesus name.

CHAPTER THREE

PRINCIPLES OF GRACIOUS SERVICE (2)

CHAPTER THREE
SUMMARY

- The Principle of Acceptable Service
- The Principle of Alignment
- The Principle of Sufficiency

"Or do you not know that your body is the temple of the Holy Spirit who is in you, whom you have from God, and you are not your own?"

2 Cor 6:19

CHAPTER THREE

PRINCIPLES OF GRACIOUS SERVICE (2)

Principle #4: The Principle of Acceptable Service.

The first thing you must learn and be conscious of about gracious service is the fact that your services will always be acceptable by God when done by grace for the kingdom. That means, it takes the enablement of grace for whatever service you render to the Lord to be accepted by Him.

For every one of us born into the kingdom of God, there is something that the Lord has brought us into the kingdom to do for Him. What has God called you to do? Are you doing what He has called you to do or are you just keeping up with the motions?

Whether it is in church, the missions field, your community or wherever the Lord has placed you in His service, the most important thing is to make sure you are doing it with the grace of God. No matter how good and noble what you do is, doing it just for the sake of doing good is not enough. It is functioning by the grace of God that sanctifies your effort before the Lord and make them count. Doing it with the consciousness that it will impact the kingdom of God is what matters most.

As you serve the purposes of God, be conscious of the grace of God at work in your life. It is a booster and a source of strength when the going gets tough. It gives energy and keeps you going even when there is no natural motivation to continue. It is the enablement that fires you up and keeps you refired for the Lord.

Some people serve just for their bellies. Others serve just to become popular or be known. Some others serve out of pride. However, God is inspiring this message in your heart now because He wants you to always remember that the underlying factor in gracious service is that your services are targeted for the kingdom of God.

In our church (DCH), we train what we call servant-leaders. So I tell everyone who passes through our Leadership Class otherwise known as workers-in-training in other parishes, that they are serving by grace, not by law. I tell them that their service is not by their enablement. So they should serve and not be afraid because there is someone who has called them and they have His backing.

PRAYER:

Father, I receive the grace to serve you acceptably at all times in Jesus name.

Principle #5: The Principle of Assignment

As believers, we are all here on an assignment given to us by our saviour and creator. We all have an assignment that we are mandated to complete within a specific time frame. That was what Paul was trying to communicate to us when he said;

"Or do you not know that your body is the temple of the Holy Spirit who is in you, whom you have from God, and you are not your own?"

1 Cor 6:19

Here is the idea ... When you gave your heart to Christ and became born again, what happened was that there was an exchange. You exchanged your life to receive His and now, as a token of ownership, His Spirit lives in you. Hence the phrase "you are not your own"

In other words, God owns you right now and He has assigned you a task to fulfil for Him over a given period.

That is why it is totally out of place to be a part of the kingdom of God and not serve in any capacity. If you are one of such believers, I have to let you know that you are wasting God's resources in your life. You are being unfruitful with His investment in your life.

Maybe you have been telling yourself that you will get serious tomorrow or you would join a ministry next week. You are the reason God asked me to write this book. You have no control over tomorrow so no need to procrastinate. You have to become time conscious, knowing that you only have so much time to fulfil your life's assignment.

"I must work the works of Him who sent Me while it is day; the night is coming when no one can work."

John 9:4

This was the reason Jesus was so effective in His earthly ministry. He had a consciousness of the fact that His assignment was time-bound. He knew that the night was coming when no one (including Jesus) would be able to work. I pray for you that you would not waste the day of your life only to realize it in the night when it is already too late.

Listen, if the very Son of God (Jesus) said He must work the works of Him that sent Him while it is still day, you can't afford to waste time. We are all on assignment, we are not here by mistake or for nothing. No one is an accident. Everyone is on assignment and that assignment can be found in Christ.

We are not going to live on this earth forever. There is a window of opportunity and availability. Whatever the service is, talk to God, the grace to do it is there. Talk to God. Live each day as though it is your last day. Ask yourself at the end of each day: *"how have I served today? Whose life did I touch today?"*

As you read this book, I pray that today will be a day of repentance in Jesus name. And if you are already serving, I pray that God will increase the grace upon you to serve. Peter and Paul did the same thing. Even Elijah knew when it was his time and he even announced it. There is a window for every one of us to serve, and I pray that we shall finish well in the name of Jesus.

PRAYER:

Lord, I receive the grace to carry out every assignment, calling and purpose you have in stock for me in Jesus name.

Principle #6: The Principle of Sufficiency

In the pursuit of your service to God, have you ever gotten to a point where it feels like you can't continue on this journey? Have you found yourself in a position where the pressure gets so much that you want to just pack up and leave?

This principle of sufficiency states that in everything, every situation and every circumstance surrounding our assignment, God's grace is always enough.

> *"And He said to me, "My grace is sufficient for you, for My strength is made perfect in weakness." Therefore most gladly I will rather boast in my infirmities, that the power of Christ may rest upon me."*

> **2 Cor 12:9**

As he journeyed towards the fulfilment of His assignment, Paul was once in a dire situation. He prayed and prayed that the Lord will take away the condition but in response, God told him that His grace was sufficient for him. No matter how weak or inadequate you may feel, always remember that there is more than enough grace available for you. I like the way The Amplified Bible expands that scripture and says;

> *"But He said to me, My grace (My favour and loving-kindness and mercy) is enough for you [sufficient against any danger and enables you to bear the trouble manfully]; for My strength and power are made perfect (fulfilled and completed) and show themselves most effective in [your]*

weakness. Therefore, I will all the more gladly glory in my weaknesses and infirmities, that the strength and power of Christ (the Messiah) may rest (yes, may pitch a tent over and dwell) upon me!"

2 Cor 12:9 [AMPC]

Wow! Grace is sufficient against ANY danger and enables you to bear the trouble manfully! This means that the only reason people quit in the assignment God has called them for is that they neglected the place of grace. They didn't take advantage of the grace of God which the Bible describes to us as being more effective in our weakness.

Think about it for a moment ...

God, knowing our frailties and the fact that we are only flesh decided of His own accord to furnish us with a spiritual resource that kicks into effect when we have exhausted ourselves! The best part is that you don't have to wait till you are exhausted to take advantage of this. In fact, you would save yourself a lot of heartache and headache by plugging into serving by grace from the get-go.

It is interesting to note that God didn't tell Paul *"my anointing, your giving, your prayers is sufficient."* He simply said, *"my grace is sufficient for you."* That's why Paul said he will glory in his infirmities. God doesn't impose Himself on anyone.

I don't know what weakness you are going through. Yes, maybe you are where God wants you to be but you are going through funny things. You need to bear in mind that the presence of challenges doesn't always mean you are out of God's place for your life.

Just remember that His grace is there to carry you through. That grace is strongest when you are weakest. For me every time I have to do something, I will tell the Lord *"I don't have the wisdom to do this, give me wisdom. I am going to rely on your strength. Lord teach me."*

Praise God, there is never a shortage or lack of grace. It now depends on how much we are ready to receive. The day I discovered this; all those things that were not working began to work. I have been saved from age 14, but it took me years to understand the power of the salvation that saved me.

After I discovered the power of grace, I went back to the things that didn't work before with the consciousness of the grace of God and began to repeat them. To the glory of God, they started working! I realized that it was not by power, it was not by might or experience but there is a place for the grace of God.

That grace was always there and I did not know. It was very scarce in the messages we heard then but thank God, those days are gone. The days of ignorance are gone. We are now in a time of refreshing. Remember grace is available to you in whatever place you are serving.

"But as you abound in everything—in faith, in speech, in knowledge, in all diligence, and in your love for us—see that you abound in this grace also."

2 Cor 8:7

You see, your love, faith, manner of speech, knowledge and hard work are great but they are not enough. Of course, you should work towards increasing in them but there is still more. You have to abound in his grace as well. As a matter of fact, all of those things are hidden in grace. Grace is a total package.

PRAYER:

Dear Father, let your grace always be sufficient for me and let your strength always be made perfect in my weakness in Jesus name

.

CHAPTER
FOUR

PRINCIPLES OF GRACIOUS
SERVICE (3)

CHAPTER FOUR SUMMARY

- The Principle of Vain Application
- The Principle of Enablement
- The Principle of Human Limitation

"Unless the Lord builds the house, They labour in vain who build it; Unless the Lord guards the city, The watchman stays awake in vain."

Psalm 127:1

CHAPTER FOUR

PRINCIPLES OF GRACIOUS SERVICE (3)

Principle #7: The Principle of Vain Application

The principle of vain application can also be referred to as the principle of zero application. It states that it is possible to receive God's grace in vain!

> *"We then, as workers together with Him also plead with you not to receive the grace of God in vain"*

2 Cor 6:1

In Paul's second book to the church in Corinth, he pleaded with them not to receive the grace of God in vain. That means it is possible to receive the grace of God in vain. It is one thing to receive the grace of God but a different ball game to use the grace that was received!

It is possible for the grace of God to be there and yet you will be labouring and struggling without results. It is possible for grace to be there and yet you are unfruitful! If you are saved, you have a measure of grace, but the question is "how are you applying it?"

It is very easy to be saved by grace and start living by the law. Some people sometimes wake up and miss their quiet time then start feeling guilty. No! No! No! it's not by law, it's by grace! He is the one that enables you. Don't let this grace be in vain. It simply means that whatever you do, it is not by your power. Remember that whatever you do, you are doing it in the name of God and for the kingdom.

It is by grace and you are not supposed to struggle for it. God has given us the grace to do it. Many of us are serving in the vineyard of God but we are doing it with a grudge, we are angry and unhappy. It sometimes feels like we are angry with God for whatever reason. It's like we are not fulfilled. The first thing you need to ask yourself is *"am I where He wants me to be?"* If the answer is yes, then you need to ask *"am I tapping into the grace He has given or am I using my wisdom."*

If you are where he wants you to be but you are trying to use your strength, you will suffer in vain. Serving God is sweet; especially if it's where he wants you to be. The day I discovered this; my mindset changed and so will yours. Praying will become interesting and teaching will become fun. And even when it is painful, you will still enjoy it because you will see that it is worth it.

It is possible to receive the grace of God in vain but I pray that will not be your portion in the mighty name of Jesus. Just look around you, who are those enjoying what they do and who are those struggling with what they do. Maybe they are not tapping into the grace of God.

PRAYER:

Dear Lord, I pray that your grace upon my life will never be in vain in Jesus name.

Principle #8: The Principle of Enablement

One of the snares of the enemy for gifted and talented people is the feeling that they are the alpha and omega of their gifts. What they fail to realize is that if estranged from the enablement of the Lord, they are nothing and can do nothing.

"Unless the Lord builds the house, They labour in vain who build it; Unless the Lord guards the city, The watchman stays awake in vain."

Psalm 127:1

The Bible tells us that it doesn't matter how skilled a builder is, the only reason he can build successfully is that God already permitted it. In other words, you can only work what the Lord has worked. If God's grace is not involved, that labour is in vain.

"For it is God which worketh in you both to will and to do of his good pleasure."

54

Php 2:13

Notice that he didn't say "unless the Lord builds the house, the builder cannot build" In other words, he didn't say men cannot make an effort when God's hand is not involved. Chances are that their efforts may even prosper for a while but in the end, it will all be an effort in futility.

Sadly, this is exactly what has happened to many people around the world. They have gone ahead of God building what God did not call them to build. They put in the work and try their best only to discover at the end that they were running in vain all along! I would rather build what God is building than run off with my agenda to discover after several years that God was not in it all the while.

PRAYER:

Lord, I receive the daily enablement to will and do your great pleasure without wavering in Jesus name.

Principle #9: The Principle of Human Limitation

One of the beautiful things about God using a man is the fact that if He required qualification from us before we could be used, no one would meet up. Man is too depraved to meet up to the standards of a Holy God. As men, we are limited to our abilities. So instead of demanding that we qualify, He becomes our qualification.

> *"And I thank Christ Jesus our Lord who has enabled me, because He counted me faithful, putting me into the ministry,"*

1 Tim 1:12

Notice that the Lord first enabled Paul before putting him into the ministry. Apart from the enablement that the Lord supplied, Paul could not be effective or productive in the ministry. What he was just saying was that God used him even as unqualified as he was! The principle of limitation states that God can use anyone even with their imperfections and limitations.

When Jesus first met Peter, he told the Lord to depart from him because he was a sinner and a man of imperfections. In fact, in just one day, Peter denied Jesus thrice in the heat of the moment but the Lord didn't count that against him. What he didn't know was that his imperfections made him perfect for Christ's grace.

PRAYER:

Lord, I know you have said you will have mercy on whom you would have mercy, Lord have mercy on me as I trust and depend on your unlimited grace in Jesus name.

CHAPTER FIVE

PRINCIPLES OF GRACIOUS SERVICE (4)

CHAPTER FIVE
SUMMARY

- The Principle of Giftings
- The Principle of Ministrations
- The Principle of Perception and Intuition

"Nevertheless, brethren, I have written more boldly to you on some points, as reminding you, because of the grace given to me by God, that I might be a minister of Jesus Christ to the Gentiles, ministering the gospel of God, that the offering of the Gentiles might be acceptable, sanctified by the Holy Spirit."
Rom 15:15-16

CHAPTER FIVE

PRINCIPLES OF GRACIOUS SERVICE (4)

Principle #10: The Principle of Giftings.

Have you ever wondered how certain gifts seem to find expression in one person's life with ease while another gift that you would consider "easier" feels difficult to them? For example, maybe you find that teaching comes naturally to you but prophesying is a high mark to hit no matter how much you pray and fast. But then, a close friend of yours seems to prophesy with ease but find it extremely difficult to teach! The grace granted to the individuals in the area of their gifting is the reason for that.

"Having then gifts differing according to the grace that is given to us, let us use them: if prophecy, let us prophesy in proportion to our faith;"

Rom 12:6

According to the Word of God, gifts differ according to the underlying grace given. The reason one person has the gift of teaching is that there is grace for teaching that has been granted to that person. The other person who seems to have the gift of administration (without studying Business Administration in college) also has that gift because a grace for administration was given to them.

In other words, what we call gifts in the physical realm is an outward manifestation of an inner supply of grace. The Bible, therefore, admonishes us to recognize and appreciate the grace of God in others while staying in our lanes.

Don't just try to copy or become something or someone else. It is better to identify what gifts you have and maximise the grace of God given you in that area.

Anyone can prophesy but not everyone is a prophet. Anyone can teach but not everyone is called to be a teacher. There is a measure of grace attached to every gift. It is that grace that sponsors the expression of the gift in your life.

> *"But to each one of us, grace was given according to the measure of Christ's gift."*

Eph 4:7

Here is another very interesting dimension to this ... Anywhere you see the word *"according,"* that means there is a level attached to it. So it means grace is given us to the measure of Christ's gift.

However, you also need to understand that having a gift in an area doesn't make it a lifetime calling. David was a shepherd, became the leader of Saul's army but was anointed to be a king. There are a lot of pastors who can sing yet they are pastors today not musicians. You can have the gift of singing but it doesn't mean you are called to be a chorister.

Whichever way, just know that for every call, there is a grace of God to back it up. If you are struggling to use a gift, you need to ask God.

"As each one has received a gift, minister it to one another, as good stewards of the manifold grace of God."

1 Pet 4:10

Now, when you have identified the gift, the Bible says to minister it to one another. Always remember that no one was given a gift for their benefit alone. Every one of us was gifted so that we can share that gift with others for the kingdom of God. The measure of your involvement in sharing it with others is what determines whether or not you are a good steward of that grace given you.

PRAYER:

Lord I know my gifting is according to your grace, help me to rely on every ounce of grace that you have given me as I function in your gifting for the purpose of the kingdom.

Principles of Gracious Service (3)

Principle #11: The Principle of Ministration

The principle of ministration states that God always backs up every assignment and ministration with His grace. It focuses on the grace to minister. If God calls someone to go minister anywhere or do something for Him, there is always the backing of grace.

> *"Nevertheless, brethren, I have written more boldly to you on some points, as reminding you, because of the grace given to me by God, that I might be a minister of Jesus Christ to the Gentiles, ministering the gospel of God, that the offering of the Gentiles might be acceptable, sanctified by the Holy Spirit."*

Rom 15:15-16

You see, Paul was aware of the supply of grace in his life and ministry. He knew that God had given him a special grace to share the gospel of Christ to the Gentiles and lead them to God. In fact, most of the other disciples didn't have an understanding of grace! That was why none of them was as effective as Paul was in ministering to the Gentile world.

You see, sometimes, when you find yourself struggling or unsettled concerning a ministration, ask yourself

65

"am I doing this by my strength or am I doing this within the scope, influence and support of the grace of God?"

Paul was able to break through and get results in the uncharted grounds of the heathen nation because he had the full backing of the grace of God on his assignment. This is the reason you find that different people do the same thing but get different results. Then you begin to ask yourself *"why is this thing easy for one and difficult for the other person?"* The point is that whatever God wants you to do, there is always the backing of His grace.

> *"Now when they had gone through Phrygia and the region of Galatia, they were forbidden by the Holy Spirit to preach the word in Asia. After they had come to Mysia, they tried to go into Bithynia, but the Spirit did not permit them. So passing by Mysia, they came down to Troas. And a vision appeared to Paul in the night. A man of Macedonia stood and pleaded with him, saying, "Come over to Macedonia and help us."*

Acts 16:6-9

Can you imagine that Paul was going to Asia to minister and the Holy Spirit, forbade them!? It caught my attention that since they were going to evangelise and preach, why will the Holy Spirit not allow them to go and preach?

What that simply means is that if they went there to go and minister against the instructions of the Holy Spirit, they were on their own. The grace of God might not be there with them because God is not the one that sent them. In other words, when you operate in the ministry in the absence of God's grace, all you are going to get eventually is dis-grace.

On another occasion, Paul and his team wanted to go to Bithynia but the Bible says that the Holy Spirit did not permit them. What Paul may not have known is that God was orchestrating the best occasion and season for his ministry.

Now, ask yourself concerning your service to the Lord for the kingdom today; *"how did I get here? Did I send myself or did God send me?"* This question explains why certain people start some things and in a short period, it is dead but others start the same thing and even amid the toughest environment and economy, they just blossom. That is because they are operating under God's grace.

I remember someone telling me that even during the global pandemic in 2020, while some churches were barely surviving because of the shutdown; some actually thrived. Some flourished during the pandemic.

It wasn't just about what they did. After all, others could have done the same things they did and not gotten the same results. There was just a backing of grace upon them. Some churches grew in online attendance! It was evident that there was an unusual release of God's grace.

The Bible further tells us that Paul was in a vision when he received a call to head to Macedonia. He yielded to that call and went to Philippi which eventually turned out to be where he had the best experience in ministry! I say that because that was the only church where he had nothing negative to say about them. The fact that the Spirit of God led him there meant that the grace of God was present to back up his work there.

Interestingly, he used a very unconventional method to start the ministry there and God backed him up. Though they got there on a Sabbath day, instead of going to the synagogue, they went to the riverside where some people usually prayed. While they were praying, a woman there heard them praying and liked what she heard. She invited them into her home and from there they had a platform and the ministry started. That is how the Book of Philippians came about.

There was so much grace there that it became the only place where Paul opened up his personal experience and released one of the biggest blessings he released in his ministry. That was where he said "... *my God will supply all your needs according to His riches in glory"* That was the only church that Paul had nothing negative to talk about. That was because there was so much grace that produced so much joy.

There is the grace of God that backs up any ministration He has commissioned. When. God's grace is there, it makes that which is difficult look so easy. Others may even want to copy it but will discover it was not as easy as it looked. That is why I always ask people *"are you sure this is what God wants you to do? Are you sure this is where God wants you to be?"*

We always have to check to see that we are where God wants us to be because that is where the grace to serve is. We don't do things just because others are doing them. We do things because there is an understanding that there is a calling, a strength and a backing of the grace of God on this ministerial assignment. Well, sometimes we step out in faith only to realise that it was a no go area. Just like Paul experienced a forbidding from the Holy Spirit.

I pray for those who are serving or desire to serve, whether it is to go on missions, to go and preach or teach or in any way you have been called to serve, I pray that you will be effective within the scope of the grace of God given unto you. May that grace make that which is difficult become easy for you in Jesus name.

PRAYER:

Lord help me never to minister or serve you on the basis of my own wisdom or knowledge, but help me to always trust in your Holy Spirit and grace in Jesus name.

Principle #12: The Principle of Perception and Intuition.

One of the most powerful things about the grace of God in a man's life is the fact that it easily reveals and announces its presence in the person's life through the outstanding result produced. When the grace of God is at work in a man's life, it has a way of making ways for him such that those who should know him get to do so easily and without forcing the discovery to happen.

Simply put, the grace of God can do a better job at marketing a person or project than any business expert can!

> *"and when James, Cephas, and John, who seemed to be pillars, perceived the grace that had been given to me, they gave me and Barnabas the right hand of fellowship, that we should go to the Gentiles and they to the circumcised."*

Gal 2:9

James, Peter and John were what you could call "senior apostles" as it were. They had physically walked with Jesus and had some first-hand training from Him. So to an extent, they were men of the Spirit and could tell when the Spirit of God was upon someone.

It is also important to note that these apostles were aware of Paul's background and antecedents in persecuting the early church. So they knew this wasn't a man who was interested in the things of Christ at all. When they saw Paul and how God was working through his life and ministry, perceived that the grace of God had been given to him. That conviction that God was at work in this the most unlikely man like Paul made them extend the right hand of fellowship to Him.

In other words, Paul didn't have to do much announcing and cajoling to the apostles. He didn't have to try to convince them that he was genuinely saved and now a servant of Jesus Christ. Somehow, something about Paul's life was screaming *"apostle of Jesus Christ"* to everyone around him.

Dear friend, grace is an announcer and can be perceived even from a distance. When it is upon a man's life, suddenly those who knew him will begin to see him in a new light. Everyone begins to call you a pastor, evangelist or teacher even without necessarily hearing you preach a sermon.

That is why you must invest your life in serving the kingdom in the area of that grace. There is something about service in the kingdom that increases that grace and its manifestation in your life. That was what happened to Jesus while He was on earth.

> *"And when the Sabbath had come, He began to teach in the synagogue. And many hearing Him were astonished, saying, "Where did this Man get these things? And what wisdom is*

this which is given to Him, that such mighty works are performed by His hands!"

Mark 6:2

For thirty years, he was just going around the place as an ordinary carpenter's son. There was nothing of worth recorded about his life except that he was in the temple arguing scriptures at age twelve. However, the moment He stepped into His calling and began to serve the purpose of God for His life, He became a New Man!

Many who heard Him teach became astonished and began to ask *"Where did this Man get these things? And what wisdom is this which is given to Him, that such mighty works are performed by His hands!"* The same fate befell the early disciples as well.

"Now when they saw the boldness of Peter and John, and perceived that they were uneducated and untrained men, they marveled. And they realized that they had been with Jesus."

Acts 4:13

After the occurrence of the healing of the lame man by the Beautiful Gate, Peter and John got into trouble with the authorities of the day. They were arrested and brought before the council to tell by what power or name they had done this work of power.

In his defence, Peter announced that it was by the name of Jesus Christ of Nazareth whom they had crucified that the man was healed. Then he went on to explain how the stone that the builders had rejected had become the chief cornerstone and that there is no other name given among men by which men can be saved.

When the leaders heard him and noted that this Peter and John didn't look like the kind of people who could have such powers, they wondered even more. In addition to that, when they observed the boldness and composure of these men who were uneducated and untrained, they knew he had to be under a superior influence. That was when they concluded that indeed this Peter must have been with Jesus.

You see, when the grace of God functions through a man's life, it makes him perform at a level beyond his level of education or training and people can always tell the difference. The grace of God is too powerful to be concealed. As you begin to serve by grace, people will begin to perceive the difference and ask questions about you too. Just make sure to always point them back to the giver of all things who has lavished His grace upon you.

I pray that the people around you will perceive God's grace upon your life and you will have space to do exploit in Jesus name.

PRAYER:

Father, I ask that you open the eyes of my understanding as I serve you, that I might see the way you saw, work the way you worked and serve the way you served in Jesus name.

CHAPTER SIX

PRINCIPLES OF GRACIOUS
SERVICE (5)

CHAPTER SIX
SUMMARY

- The Principle of Compensation
- The Principle of the End
- The Principle of Accomplishment

"knowing that from the Lord you will receive the reward of the inheritance; for[a] you serve the Lord Christ. 25 But he who does wrong will be repaid for what he has done, and there is no partiality."
Col 3:24

CHAPTER SIX

PRINCIPLES OF GRACIOUS SERVICE (5)

Principle #13: The Principle of Compensation.

This principle simply states that there is compensation for every service, work and everything that we do for God by His grace.

> *"And behold, I am coming quickly, and My reward is with Me, to give to every one according to his work."*

Rev. 22:12

Everything that we do for God has a reward and compensation. God does not owe any man. He always has a reward according to what we have done for Him. God is not an employer that uses people and dumps them. He is someone that even before we begin to serve Him, He already told us that "if we are willing and obedient, we shall eat the good of the land" (Isa 1:19) Now, sometimes, what is a reward to one person may not be a reward to someone else.

"And so it was, because the midwives feared God, that He provided households for them."

Exo. 1:21

Remember the example of those midwives that Pharoah had told to kill all male children that would be born? The Bible says that because they feared God and refused to carry out Pharoah's bidding, God rewarded them with households.

I know that for some people, households may not be a reward but that was God's compensation for these women. I believe that God must have seen that the only way these women could have their own families was going to be by a miracle that only God could perform!

80

That was why God came up strong for them in that area of life.

The Bible also talks about the fact that "… children are a heritage from the Lord, the fruit of the womb is a reward." (Psalm 127:3). A reward is something that you are given as a result of what you have done.

God told Abraham that He is a sure rewarder whose reward is guaranteed. He doesn't tell us to obey Him for nothing. There is always something at the end of it. However, this is not to say we should have the mindset of entitlement.

> *"knowing that from the Lord you will receive the reward of the inheritance; for[a] you serve the Lord Christ. 25 But he who does wrong will be repaid for what he has done, and there is no partiality."*

Col 3:24

Whatever you do in service to the Lord in HIs vineyard, the Bible enjoins us to do it as unto the Lord because He is the one that will reward us. We are told to know that it is from the Lord that we will receive the reward of inheritance. That means there is an inheritance to receive for the service that we render to the Lord.

While speaking to his disciples, one time, Jesus said "... *I go to prepare a place for you and I will come again and receive you to Myself ...*" That is also part of the reward!

Now, let me state categorically that this reward is not only in heaven. There are rewards that we enjoy on earth as a result of what we do for the Lord. Remember those servants? The Lord told them "... welcome, you faithful and good servants"

> *"Now he who plants and he who waters are one, and each one will receive his own reward according to his own labour."*

1 Cor 3:8

There is no committee of rewards or group rewards! Every man shall receive his reward according to what he has done.

The Bible talks about an account where a man was recruiting people at different hours of the day in Matthew Chapter 20. In the end, he gave each of them a reward based on what they had done. God's reward system differs from man's. He sees the heart of men and decides what reward to give to everyone accordingly.

"So Jesus said to them, "Assuredly I say to you, that in the regeneration, when the Son of Man sits on the throne of His glory, you who have followed Me will also sit on twelve thrones, judging the twelve tribes of Israel."

Matt 19:28

Although Jesus was talking directly to His early disciples here, the same applies to each one of us too. We are going to be part of the judges.

"And everyone who has left houses or brothers or sisters or father or mother [a] or wife or children or lands, for My name's sake, shall receive a hundredfold, and inherit eternal life."

Matt. 19:29

He refers to those who have turned their homes into places where God dwells and have made God the priority in their lives over all else. When there is a conflict between what people want you to do and what God wants you to do, how do you handle the situation? Jesus said if you make God your priority and prioritize all others for His sake, you will receive a hundredfold on this earth.

What this hundredfold represents will vary greatly from person to person. Just like Hannah gave up Samuel for the work of the kingdom and God blessed her with five more children! Maybe it is your land you gave up, your comfort or your time. Whatever it is that you have laid down for the love of God and the kingdom, He will repay in Heaven's definition.

Whatever we do for God, there is always a reward. It pays to serve God. It pays to walk with God. It pays to love God and work for Him. He is the best employer, the best Master, He is the best manager. He is the pastor of pastors and the leader of leaders. He is the one that we are actually working for.

Consequently, if anyone gives you any instruction that contradicts what God has told you, default to God. Paul said, *"Imitate me, just as I also imitate Christ."* (1 Cor 11:1). In other words, Christ is the reference point.

Yes, man can reward us but man is limited in what they can do. A man can only give you out of what God enables them to give you. When God rewards, on the other hand, He is not someone that will come back and make a fool of you afterwards. When God rewards, everyone will know that this is God! Every eye will see it and acknowledge that this is the doing of the Lord and it is marvellous in our sight.

So remember, as you serve God through grace for the kingdom of God, you are not serving in vain. He is a faithful God who is also loving, wonderful and glorious. Time will fail me to share the testimonies of what God has done in my life as I serve Him.

> *"looking unto Jesus, the author and finisher of our faith, who for the joy that was set before Him endured the cross, despising the shame, and has sat down at the right hand of the throne of God."*

Heb 12:2

Jesus despised the shame and endured the cross because He had the end in mind. Eventually, He is seated at the right hand of God the Father! It is always best to serve God with an end in mind; knowing fully well that God is there to lead, guide and walk with you to the end.

Always remember that God is a rewarder. He is not a wicked God. He is a just God. It is only men that can despitefully use people. It is only men that can shame people. God is faithful. When you serve Him in spirit and truth, He will make sure that He takes care of you.

So when God says follow me, He is saying "... I am responsible for your upkeep, protection and provision" Following God simply means watching and serving Him. One of the best things about the grace to serve is that God doesn't just give us the grace to serve, He rewards us for serving Him by the grace He gave to us.

I pray for you that as you have read this book that you get involved with serving the Lord, may He reward you beyond your imagination in Jesus name.

PRAYER:

Lord on that day when you shall make the roll call in heaven, may I not be found wanting or missing. I shall receive all the crowns that you have reserved for those you have called and who walked according to your will in Jesus name.

Principle #14: The Principle of the End

As we talk about the grace to serve, it is important to bear in mind that the *"principle of the end"* states that everything that has a beginning on this earth has an end

86

too. Whether good or bad, on this plane of human existence, everything that has a beginning also has an end.

Nothing lasts forever. No matter how great it is, an end is coming. When Christ comes, everything will end and a new era will begin because there is something better in heaven.

You might be wondering, *"what does this have to do with grace?"* The Bible says that there is time for everything on earth.

> *"To everything there is a season, a time for every purpose under heaven:"*

Eccl 3:1

There is a time to be born and a time to die. Everything we do on this earth has a time scope. There is a window of time given for every purpose on the earth and that includes the use of the grace given to you. So whether we like it or not, an end is going to come. It's either we go to meet Jesus Christ or He comes to meet us. Whichever way, an end will come.

When that end finally comes, no one can use the grace given them to serve again. No one can add or subtract from what he has already done. We are all going to account for what we have done on earth. Every one of us will give account for what we did with the grace of God that was bestowed upon us.

> *"His lord said to him, 'Well done, good and faithful servant; you have been faithful over a few things, I will make you ruler over many things. Enter into the joy of your lord."*

Matt 25:23

The word "faithful" in the above scripture means that you have served faithfully. That tells you something … We are going to be rewarded as servants, not as sons at the return of the Lord!

It is not enough to be saved. You have to serve. If you are saved and you are not participating in anything of benefit to the kingdom, this is the time to arise and take part in kingdom service. The Bible could have said *"good and faithful son."* Rather, it says "good and faithful servant."

Another way to describe service here is our worship and our commitment. Remember when the children of Israel were about to leave Egypt, God told Moses to tell Pharaoh to let His people go that they may serve Him. You were saved, delivered and liberated to serve God with everything you have. You see, your finances, your home and whatever thing that He has given unto you are for service to Him.

If you are not doing that, then you are missing out on so much. Your reward at the end of the day is a function of how much of this grace given to you was applied. It is a measure of how well you have served in the time and space given to you.

An end is coming whether we like it or not. I pray that you will not die young in Jesus name. I pray you will live long, till 120 years if Christ tarries. But at the end of that, do you want to be received as a good and faithful servant or do you want to be rejected as a bad and unfaithful servant? My prayer is that you would be part of those to be received as faithful servants in Jesus name.

God gave us His grace to serve. That is why He gave us the great commission to go forth and teach every nation. He said to go and preach the gospel of the kingdom to every creature. We were saved to serve.

> *"You did not choose Me, but I chose you and appointed you that you should go and bear fruit and that your fruit should*

remain, that whatever you ask the Father in My name He may give you."

John 15:16

You see, just as God saved us to serve, with that mandate to serve came the enablement to do so as well. He appointed and graced us to go and bear abiding fruits. That means He made available to us the necessary endowment to get results. So at the end of time, it is only fair for Him to find out from you what you did with all that investment.

PRAYER:

Lord, I receive the grace to redeem the time as I serve you. I receive the grace to work while it is still day in Jesus name.

Principle #15: The Principle of Accomplishment

As a child of God, you should know that you cannot become all that God has created you to become without the presence of His grace. You need His grace to fulfil the purpose for which you were created. Severed from that grace, all your efforts and attempts will only be in futility.

However, that is not to say that grace is an excuse for laziness; far from it! You have a role to play. When you apply the grace of God to what you do, the result will be outstanding and people will wonder how you were able to do it.

If there is anyone in the Bible who understood the concept of grace and enjoyed it well, it is Paul. Coming from a religious background and being one of the greatest persecutors of the church, you would think he would be the last person God would call. He even referred to himself as being less than the least of all saints!

> *"To me, who am less than the least of all the saints, this grace was given, that I should preach among the Gentiles the unsearchable riches of Christ,"*

Eph 3:8

Notice that even though he was probably the least qualified by human standards, grace still distinguished Paul. Grace reached out to him and made up for his inadequacies and insufficiencies. He would later say;

"But by the grace of God I am what I am, and His grace toward me was not in vain, but I laboured more abundantly than they all, yet not I, but the grace of God which was with me."

1 Cor. 15:10

What turned an injurious terrorist (in today's parlance) into one of the foremost apostles of the early church was grace. What made a persecutor of the disciples become the one through whom two-thirds of the New Testament section of the Bible was written was grace.

It doesn't matter your background right now or how far away you are from the fulfilment of the call of God upon your life. Grace is the principle of accomplishment. It is the vehicle for the fulfilment of all destinies.

Like Paul, whatever you will become in Christ is hidden in the envelope of grace. He is the one that makes and he is the one that breaks. If you have given your life to Him, He is the one that will enable you to do all He has destined you for.

"So he answered and said to me: "This is the word of the Lord to Zerubbabel: 'Not by might nor by power, but by My Spirit,' Says the Lord of hosts."

Zech 4:6

The accomplishment of your divine assignment will not be by your efforts. It will not be by works, might or experience either. The Bible says one thing that must be present in the equation of the accomplishment of your destiny is the grace of God. Two hundred people can prepare for a race, but something can go wrong. Time and chance will determine the eventual outcome!

As you read this book right now, there is a measure of grace bestowed upon you. It is that grace that has led you to read this book in the first place. What Paul was trying to tell us was that *"when it was time to pray, he prayed. When it was time to fast, he fasted. When it was time to go clean chairs, he did that. When it was time to go for evangelism, he did too."* Then he added that it was not just him that did those things but the grace of God that was at work in his life.

In other words, grace wasn't entirely the absence of work in Paul's life. Rather, it was the enablement to do what needed to be done for destiny to be fulfilled.

Some time ago, I was talking to a group of nurses about their work I found out that for some of them, nursing was like a headache. It was just too much trouble for them but they were just doing it for the money. Whereas, some others were doing it as though it was their calling. For this second group, it was like a life assignment!

Remember there is grace for everything God has called you to do. If you find yourself struggling to do what God has called you to do, maybe you need to check yourself. Maybe you are not following the great manual "the Bible" or you are not doing it the way God has called you to do it.

Wherever you are today is by the grace of God. Whatever you have accomplished for the kingdom of God, it is grace that has enabled you. I have heard people say they fasted for forty days and forty nights and then received power!

No! First, it was God who gave you the grace to fast and pray. And because you did it, He added more grace to you. It doesn't start with you. It started with God. So check yourself. Why are you struggling? Are you trying to do it alone or with God? Let God in on the journey with you and enjoy victory and accomplishment on a different level!

PRAYER:

94

Dear Father, I receive the grace to finish well and finish strong in Jesus name.

CHAPTER SEVEN

CONCLUSION

CHAPTER SEVEN
SUMMARY

"So Jesus said to them, "Assuredly I say to you, that in the regeneration, when the Son of Man sits on the throne of His glory, you who have followed Me will also sit on twelve thrones, judging the twelve tribes of Israel. And everyone who has left houses or brothers or sisters or father or mother [b]or wife or children or lands, for My name's sake, shall receive a hundredfold, and inherit eternal life. But many who are first will be last, and the last first."

Matt 19:28-30

CHAPTER SEVEN

CONCLUSION

In conclusion, there is a grace to serve. God is not someone that will tell you to go and do something without doing it with you. He said, *"I will be with you till the end of the age"* (Matthew 28:20) He never leaves us, He never forsakes us. He is not only there with us, His grace is also there.

Wherever God is, His grace abounds and whatever He tells us to do, whether through the calling, our gifting or whichever area that we serve, He backs us up with His grace.

I hope and pray that as you serve in the vineyard, you will have it at the back of your mind that all the help you need is available in the grace of God. He will not forsake or leave you. He will always be there.

As you serve Him, do it with joy, love and the best of the grace that He has given unto you. Don't give God *"half-baked bread"* service! Go all the way. Serve Him with the whole of your heart, soul and spirit. Remember, He will surely reward you. Not only in heaven but even on earth as well.

If you have not been serving, as you have read this book, I pray that you will be encouraged, and motivated to start doing so, even as you ask Him for what He wants you to do and trust Him to lead you to the right place to serve accordingly. May His grace be made abundantly available to you as begin to serve in Jesus name.

If you have been serving God half-heartedly – *giving half-baked bread kind of service* – I pray you will repent and begin to render acceptable service to Him in Jesus name.

Finally, I pray that on that day, everyone who had laboured acceptably, still laboring now and those that will so labor in future may hear the voice *"well done, you faithful and good servant, you have been faithful in little, I am going to bless you with this much"*

I believe that you have been blessed reading this book. Please share the revealed truth therein with as many as you can. Don't keep it to yourself. May the Lord bless and keep you in Jesus name.

Bear in mind that you will one day stand in front of Christ whom you are serving. In whichever area you are led to serve, we are all one. We were created to serve and there is a reward for serving by grace.

> *"So Jesus said to them, "Assuredly I say to you, that in the regeneration, when the Son of Man sits on the throne of His glory, you who have followed Me will also sit on twelve thrones, judging the twelve tribes of Israel. And everyone who has left houses or brothers or sisters or father or mother [h]or wife or children or lands, for My name's sake, shall receive a hundredfold, and inherit eternal life. But many who are first will be last, and the last first."*

Matt. 19:28-30

There is a reward for you here on earth. God owes no man. He is a rewarder of them that diligently serve

Him. He is a faithful employer. You don't need to die before you reap your reward. I pray that for your service to the Lord here in this world, may your reward not pass you by in Jesus name.

Assignment, Calling and Purpose

1.) *An assignment* is a task or piece of work assigned to someone as part of a job or course of study. (Oxford Dictionary) A spiritual assignment is a task or a piece of work assigned to a believer in the kingdom. It is sometimes temporary, short spaced, specific and could be otherwise. It can also lead to the primary calling of a Christian.

We can find examples in the lives of Joseph (Gen 37:14), Saul (1 Samuel 9:3) and David (1 Sam 17:17) who were sent on assignments by their parents but that led them into the call of God upon their lives.

"Then He called His twelve disciples together and gave them power and authority over all demons, and to cure diseases."

Luke 9:1

"Go therefore and make disciples of all the nations, baptizing them in the name of the Father and of the Son

Conclusion

*and of the Holy Spirit, 20 teaching them to observe all
things that I have commanded you; and lo, I am with you
always, even to the end of the age." Amen."*

Matt 28:19-20

In Luke 9:1, Jesus sent forth the disciples to go and
preach. At that time, it was a short term assignment, but
by the time we get to Matt 28:19-20, it had become a
long term assignment or what we can refer to as a
global assignment for every believer.

2.)   *A calling* is specific to an individual. According
to Merriam-webster dictionary, it is a strong inner
impulse toward a particular course of action especially
when accompanied by conviction of divine influence.

A spiritual calling might be tied to our spiritual giftings,
skills or talents.

"For the gifts and the calling of God are irrevocable."

Rom 11:29

The scripture above confirms that spiritual callings and
giftings are without repentance. God gives them for life
for His kingdom. There is a specific calling upon the life
of every individual. According to 1 Cor. 7:20, the Bible

103

says *"Let every man abide in the same calling wherein he was called."*

For example, Paul would always refer to himself as someone called to be an apostle of Jesus Christ according to Rom 1:1, but the truth is that we are not all called to be apostles. So this call was unique to Paul.

> *"And God has appointed these in the church: first apostles, second prophets, third teachers, after that miracles, then gifts of healings, helps, administrations, varieties of tongues."*

1 Cor 12:28

According to the Word of God, some of us are called to be teachers, prophets, administrators, etc based on our spiritual giftings. These callings are pre-ordained. We discover them, we don't create them. There is a general call into the kingdom of God through the leading of the Holy Spirit for everyone. This is the call that leads to salvation.

> *"Before I formed you in the womb I knew you; Before you were born I sanctified you; I ordained you a prophet to the nations."*

Jer. 1:5

3.)   *Purpose* on the other hand is defined by the Oxford Dictionary as the reason for which something is done or created or for which something exists. As believers we have one primary purpose in Christ, to spend the rest of our lives with Him in Heaven. Everything else points towards this. Therefore, whatever we do should be in line with His purpose.

"For God so loved the world that He gave His only begotten Son, that whoever believes in Him should not perish but have everlasting life."

John 3:16

"And we know that all things work together for good to those who love God, to those who are the called according to His purpose."

Romans 8:28

"But you are a chosen generation, a royal priesthood, a holy nation, His own special people, that you may proclaim the praises of Him who called you out of darkness into His marvelous light;"

1 Peter 2:9

However, in walking towards His purpose, each one of us as believers may also discover our unique purposes which sometimes could stem up from our assignments or callings.

DID YOU ENJOY THIS BOOK?

Did you enjoy reading this book? Do you know someone that can benefit from it? Feel free to share it with them with the following link: https://lasouchpublishing.com/oluBOlumuyiwa/grace

I would appreciate it if you take a moment and leave an honest review for this book on Amazon. This helps others find the book and decide if this is a fit for them.

PRAYER OF SALVATION

Heavenly Father, I thank you for loving me so much and sending your Son Jesus to die for me so that I might be saved. Dear Lord Jesus, I acknowledge my sins and confess them right now.

I declare that you are LORD over my life from this moment forward. Thank you Father for saving me, in Jesus name.

Amen.

CONTACT THE AUTHOR

Olu B. Olumuyiwa

Email: oolumuyiwa@gmail.com

Website: https://www.olubolumuyiwa.com

THE
AUTHOR

ABOUT THE AUTHOR

Olu B. Olumuyiwa is a gifted poet, prolific writer and a detailed teacher of the Word of God with a special revelation on the in-depth and true meaning of the Grace of God through Jesus Christ.

He is the author of the book "The Grace Factor" and has also written so many Christian literature and articles. He loves to teach, mentor, empower and train others to live to their fullest capacity by taking advantage of the Grace of God in Christ Jesus.

A graduate of Electrical Electronics Engineering from the University of Ibadan, Nigeria, he also has two Masters degrees in Computer Science from Texas Southern University and Business Administration from the University of Houston, Texas.

He is currently a Lead Technology Consultant in one of the largest global IT industries after several years of practice as a Lead Network Engineer in one of the largest global Oil and Gas servicing companies in the world.

He is also an Associate Pastor at RCCG Dominion Chapel Houston Parish where he is currently in charge of all the discipleship and prayer ministries.

Pastor Olu lives with his family in the US.

You can connect with Olu B. Olumuyiwa on social media through any of the following channels.

Facebook: The Grace Factor Facebook Page

Instagram: @oolumuyiwa2017

Made in the USA
Monee, IL
24 May 2022

96993620R00069